COOKING CHEMISTRY
WHY DOES GELATIN JIGGLE?

by India James

pogo

Ideas for Parents and Teachers

Pogo Books let children practice reading informational text while introducing them to nonfiction features such as headings, labels, sidebars, maps, and diagrams, as well as a table of contents, glossary, and index.

Carefully leveled text with a strong photo match offers early fluent readers the support they need to succeed.

Before Reading

- "Walk" through the book and point out the various nonfiction features. Ask the student what purpose each feature serves.
- Look at the glossary together. Read and discuss the words.

During Reading

- Have the child read the book independently.
- Invite them to list questions that arise from reading.

After Reading

- Discuss the child's questions. Talk about how they might find answers to those questions.
- Prompt the child to think more. Ask: Have you ever eaten a gelatin dessert? What did it look like when it moved?

Pogo Books are published by Jump!
3500 American Blvd W, Suite 150
Bloomington, MN 55431
www.jumplibrary.com

Copyright © 2026 Jump!
International copyright reserved in all countries.
No part of this book may be reproduced in any form without written permission from the publisher.

Jump! is a division of FlutterBee Education Group.

Library of Congress Cataloging-in-Publication Data

Names: James, India, author.
Title: Why does gelatin jiggle? / by India James.
Description: Minneapolis, MN: Jump!, Inc., [2026]
Series: Cooking chemistry | Includes index.
Audience: Ages 7-10
Identifiers: LCCN 2025008668 (print)
LCCN 2025008669 (ebook)
ISBN 9798892138468 (hardcover)
ISBN 9798892138475 (paperback)
ISBN 9798892138482 (ebook)
Subjects: LCSH: Gelatin–Juvenile literature.
Collagen–Juvenile literature.
Gelation–Juvenile literature.
Refrigerated desserts–Juvenile literature.
Classification: LCC TX553.P7 J28 2026 (print)
LCC TX553.P7 (ebook)
DDC 641.86/42–dc23/eng/20250429
LC record available at https://lccn.loc.gov/2025008668
LC ebook record available at https://lccn.loc.gov/202

Editor: Katie Chanez
Designer: Anna Peterson

Photo Credits: Oleksiy Rybakov/Shutterstock, cover; instamatics/iStock, 1; nito/Shutterstock, 3; Africa Studio/Shutterstock, 4, 12-13 (background), 16-17 (foreground), 23; ajcespedes/iStock, 5 (gelatin); Adhi Syailendra/iStock, 5 (child); HandmadePictures/iStock, 6; Krakenimages/Shutterstock, 7 (foreground); Billion Photos/Shutterstock, 7 (background); Science Photo Library/Alamy, 8-9; New Africa/Shutterstock, 10-11, 12-13 (powder); imageBROKER/Alamy, 11; DROBOT VIKTORIIA/Shutterstock, 14-15; KB Focused Imagery/Shutterstock, 16-17 (background); Diane Labombarbe/iStock, 18 (recipe card); Steve Cukrov/Shutterstock, 18 (apple juice); Anna Peterson, 19; Carolyn Franks/Shutterstock, 20 (top); Shutterstock, 20 (bottom); Katie Chanez, 21.

Printed in the United States of America at Corporate Graphics in North Mankato, Minnesota.

TABLE OF CONTENTS

CHAPTER 1
Dancing Dessert 4

CHAPTER 2
Making the Jiggle 6

CHAPTER 3
Let's Cook! 18

ACTIVITIES & TOOLS
Try This! 22
Glossary 23
Index 24
To Learn More 24

CHAPTER 1

DANCING DESSERT

Joey eats a **gelatin** dessert. It is bright red. The **flavor** is strawberry.

Joey scoops it with a spoon. It jiggles! Its **texture** is smooth and slippery. Yum!

CHAPTER 1 5

CHAPTER 2
MAKING THE JIGGLE

Gelatin desserts come in many flavors and colors. They can be made in **molds**. These give them fun shapes. Some people add fruit or other foods!

These desserts are made with gelatin powder. This makes the desserts jiggle. What is gelatin? How does it make food wobble? Let's learn!

CHAPTER 2 | 7

Gelatin is an **ingredient**. It is made from **collagen**. This is a **protein**. Collagen **molecules** look like three springs twisted together. This makes collagen **elastic**. It stretches and bounces back.

> **DID YOU KNOW?**
>
> Gelatin is a semisolid. This means it is not as **firm** as a solid.

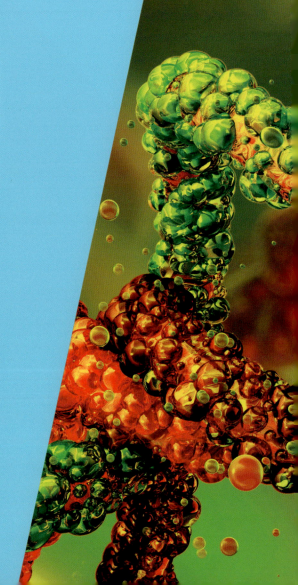

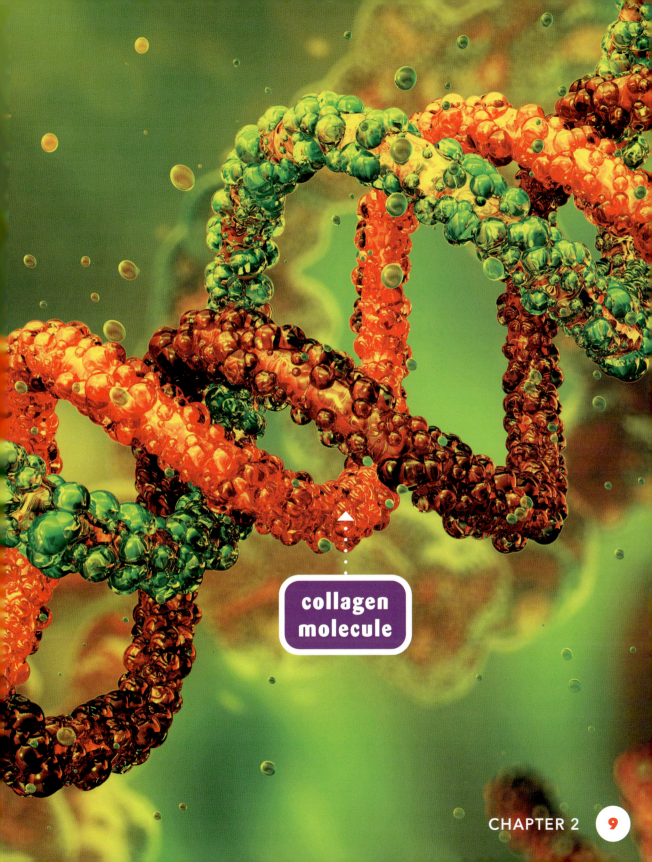

CHAPTER 2

Gelatin often comes from cows and pigs. It is made from their skin and bones. Why? These parts have a lot of collagen. They are ground up to make powder.

Agar-agar is a gelatin **substitute**. It can be used like gelatin. But it is not made from animals. It is made from seaweed!

agar-agar powder

CHAPTER 2 11

The collagen powder is mixed with **acid**. The springs untangle. This is gelatin. Then the mixture is dried. It is ground into another powder. This is gelatin powder. It is mixed with hot water.

DID YOU KNOW?

Gelatin is found in many **products**. It gives them a smooth texture. Gum and pudding are two.

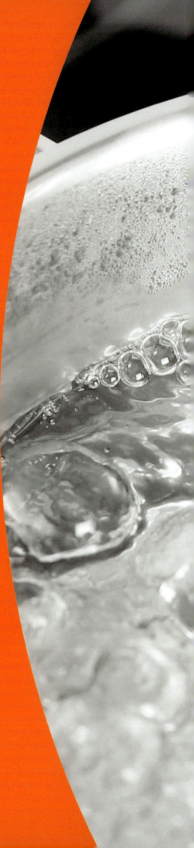

gelatin powder

CHAPTER 2

The gelatin cools and becomes firm. The water is trapped. It pushes on the gelatin molecules when you shake it. The gelatin jiggles!

TAKE A LOOK!

Why does gelatin jiggle? Take a look!

1 Collagen molecules are long, twisted springs.

2 Collagen powder is mixed with acid. The molecules untangle. This is gelatin.

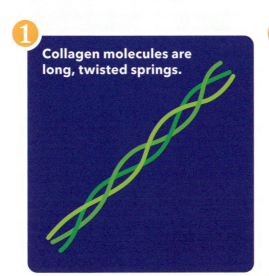
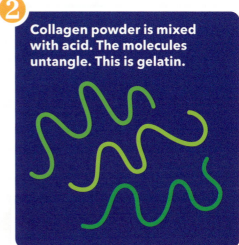

3 Gelatin powder mixes with hot water. The water is trapped between gelatin molecules.

4 The water stops the gelatin from becoming solid. It jiggles.

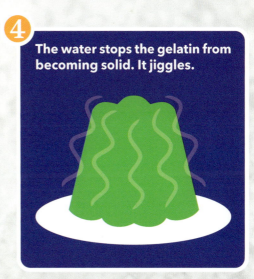

CHAPTER 2

16 CHAPTER 2

Gelatin is clear. It has no taste. We add sugar, flavor, and food coloring. This makes gelatin desserts bright and tasty!

DID YOU KNOW?

Jell-O is a popular gelatin dessert. It was **invented** in 1845. It comes in more than 15 flavors!

CHAPTER 2

CHAPTER 3
LET'S COOK!

You can make a gelatin dessert! Ask an adult for help.

GELATIN DESSERT

INGREDIENTS
- ¾ cup (180 milliliters) fruit juice
- ½ tablespoon (9 grams) gelatin powder
- ¼ cup (60 mL) water

KITCHEN TOOLS
- mixing bowl
- fork
- pot
- small dish

START WITH THESE STEPS:

1

Pour ¼ cup (59 mL) of fruit juice into the mixing bowl.

2

Add the gelatin powder. Mix with a fork.

CHAPTER 3 19

3

With an adult's help, boil ¼ cup (59 mL) of water in a pot.

4

Add the hot water and the rest of the juice to the bowl. Mix the ingredients.

20 CHAPTER 3

5

Pour it into a small dish. Chill for three hours.

6

Slice and eat your treat!

CHAPTER 3 21

ACTIVITIES & TOOLS

TRY THIS!

SHAPING GELATIN

Gelatin powder mixed with hot water is liquid. When it cools, it becomes semisolid. This means it can be shaped. See how in this fun activity!

What You Need:
- 1¾ cup (414 mL) water
- 3 ounces (85 g) flavored gelatin powder
- pot
- bowl
- food-safe mold
- plate

1. Boil 1 cup (237 mL) of water in a pot.
2. Mix the boiling water and gelatin powder in a bowl.
3. Add ¾ cup (177 mL) cold water to the mixture.
4. Pour the mixture into the mold.
5. Chill until the gelatin dessert is semisolid.
6. Turn the mold over onto a plate. Shake the mold if needed.
7. Enjoy the jiggly treat!

GLOSSARY

acid: A substance with a sour taste that reacts to a base to form a salt.

collagen: A protein in the body that is used to build skin, muscles, bones, and other tissues.

elastic: Able to stretch and return to its original shape.

firm: Solid.

flavor: Taste.

gelatin: A clear substance made from animal bones and other tissues.

ingredient: An item used to make something.

invented: Created and produced for the first time.

molds: Shaped containers that liquids are poured into to set in that shape.

molecules: The smallest units that chemicals can be divided into.

products: Things that are manufactured.

protein: A nutrient that is found in all living things and is necessary for life.

substitute: Something used in place of another.

texture: The way something feels.

ACTIVITIES & TOOLS

INDEX

acid 12, 15
agar-agar 11
animals 11
collagen 8, 11, 12, 15
firm 8, 14
flavor 4, 6, 17
food coloring 17
fruit 6
gelatin dessert 4, 6, 7, 17, 18
gelatin powder 7, 12, 15, 18, 19

ingredient 8, 18, 20
Jell-O 17
jiggles 5, 7, 14, 15
juice 18, 19, 20
molds 6
protein 8
semisolid 8
sugar 17
texture 5, 12
water 12, 14, 15, 18, 20

TO LEARN MORE

Finding more information is as easy as 1, 2, 3.

1. Go to www.factsurfer.com
2. Enter "gelatin" into the search box.
3. Choose your book to see a list of websites.